Chains Around My Soul: Between Shadows & Light

Dear Uncle Wayne,
I pray you enjoy my
first compilation of poetry
Enjoy
Love,
Vernie Lynn

VL Parker

Copyright © 2013 VL Parker

All rights reserved.

:

DEDICATION

To my husband Robert, your love has healed me and to my God for saving me from despair and darkness.

**Love heals all wounds and God is
Love**

"For with thee is the
fountain of life:
in thy light shall we
see light"
(Psalm 36: 9)

May the Light of
Love make the
darkness
diminish

CONTENTS

#	TITLE	P#
1	ACKNOWLEDGMENTS	8
2	A LIGHT IN THE DARKNESS	9
3	A THORN IN MY SIDE	11
4	**ACCEPTING ME**	13
5	ALONE BENEATH THE STARS	15
6	ALPHABETICAL ALLEGATIONS AND REPRIEVE	16
7	AN EAGLE'S CRY	17
8	ANATHEMATIZED	19
9	AUTUMN LEAVES	20
10	BETWEEN LIGHT AND SHADOWS	22
11	CAN YOU HEAR HIS VOICE	24
13	CHAINS AROUND MY SOUL	25
14	FOLLOW ME	27
15	GROWING GREY	30
16	I WAIT FOR DEATH & DEATH WAITS FOR ME	33
17	IF	35

18	INSIDE OUT	38
19	NO LONGER YOUR APHRODITE	40
20	OCEAN BLUES	43
21	ON MY OWN	46
22	ONCE I WAS A LADY	49
23	PRISONER OF TIME	52
24	REACHING FOR HIS HAND	54
25	REST IN PEACE	56
26	RIDE LIKE THE WIND	61
27	SALVATION'S COME	62
28	SHADOWS OF MY MIND	64
29	SOMETHING ISN'T RIGHT	66
30	STANDING ON A PRECIPICE	70
31	TAKE A STAND	72
32	THE HOUR'S PAST	75
33	THE ROAD I'VE TAKEN	78
34	WAR INSIDE OF ME	82
35	WHERE ONLY SHADOWS RESIDE	84
36	WICKED	86
37	YESTERDAY'S CHILD	90

Chains Around My Soul: Between Shadows & Light

38	YOU ARE	92
39	ZENITH	96
	ABOUT THE AUTHOR	98
40	" PARENTHETICAL"	100

ACKNOWLEDGMENTS

Thank you to God, Robert, Matthew, Sarah & Jessica. Your love has helped deliver me from darkness and set my soul free.

Your love has not only brought healing; it has helped shape me into who I am and encouraged me to pursue my dreams. Thank you.

A LIGHT IN THE DARKNESS

Looking for a light to see
No one here to comfort me
The Moon is bright
A Cold, barren luminosity

I'm a child of the Moon and the Sea
Longing for a Star to guide me
The storm has gripped my soul tonight
Darkness let me be

Shadows my past I see
Return to the Sea, the Sea
I'll reach for the candle in the night, a little warmth
…a little light
Blown about with a breeze to guide me

A day will come when Death does call me
Be free, be free
I see it shining in what's right
In thy Light I see, luminosity

1984

VL Parker

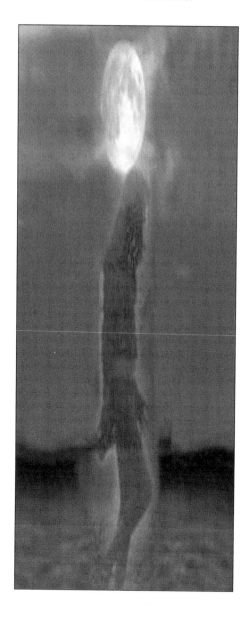

A THORN IN MY SIDE

Anger seethes inside my mind
Filled with heartache, filled with fear
Running from the child I left behind
Fleeing across the years

Will the anger ever end?
You are the one who lied, denied
There is nowhere left to run, so why pretend?
Just a painful memory inside, I hide

A thorn forever in my side
Piercing in my mind
After I have cried
Hit rewind

My shell is cracked
It crumbles away
I know today I felt attacked
I'm broken, but please stay

The spark lit a fire on this stormy night
A distorted passion I cannot fight
The flame will burn, nothing's wrong
The candle now has burned for far too long

Memories still haunt me
But I don't know why
Love can set me free
So in the dark I lie, I lie

A thorn forever in my side
Piercing in my mind

VL 1987

VL Parker

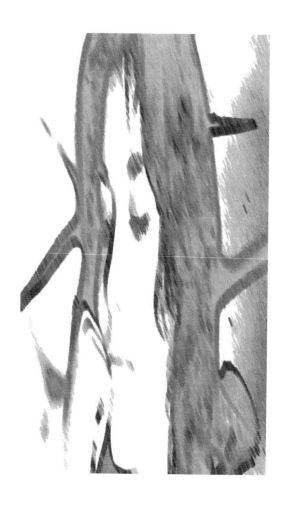

ACCEPTING ME

Why, is the question we all ask
Dwelling on something from the past
Wondering why it had to happen to us,
Always making a great big fuss
Feeling sorry for ourselves is easy
Not facing reality.

Face the truth and realize maybe,
It was meant to be
Face the facts,
Without dwelling on the past
Maybe it was an accident
Or maybe man is bent

You can't change the past, nor what went wrong
Find yourself and be strong
You survived the fight
Now you're all grown, do what's right

And don't repeat your parents' mistakes
Otherwise it will be you your kids hate.
No one will believe in you
Unless you start believing too

1987

ALONE BENEATH THE STARS

My
Cross
No prayer
No candle
Still I know he's watching me from on high
I hear a gentle laugh, with a reassuring sigh
I sit alone beneath the stars shedding tears
I look for light in darkness, still I fear
The shadows that I cannot erase
I am not able to seek your face
No sword no shield no armor for this fight
I hang my head to cry until I gain my sight
I feel my spirit freed from this earthly place
I sense acceptance
I feel your peace
At last tranquility
As I drift into
Endless
Sleep

ALPHABETICAL ALLEGATIONS AND REPRIEVE

I once was afflicted and in pain
Belittled with a broken heart and battered soul
I couldn't be candid, I was just a child
I was defective, damaged deep inside

Knowing my faith eroded when I couldn't stop the rain
Feeling I was felled too far, lost with no control
Too long I grieved the death of the child left defiled
I was too horrified… I could not abide

As children we're imprisoned, sure to go insane
I was also judged… life took its toll
I felt you kicked me to the ground, so I went wild
I laughed, I lived and loved, still, I died

When married and mended I held you with disdain
Thankful I was new and Love made me whole
I was capable, open and no longer riled
My Love now protected me, I didn't have to hide

Now I'm a queen and with my King who will reign
Living like I'm royalty since he saved my soul
I am now sanctified, somewhat meek and mild
Though I am tenacious because for me he died

I never felt understood, still he washed away the stain
Victory made me vivacious… I am in control
I am now wise, lessons that compiled
A little bit xenophobic when it comes to men, but I no longer
have to hide

I am forever young without feeling the strain
Some say I'm zealous for life, for love; I finally have a soul, I'm
whole, I'm whole

AN EAGLE'S CRY

I hear the eagle screech at the break of day
It is calling out my name; I pray

I hear a distant sound carried by the Wind
It is singing out your song; I sinned

I feel the river washing over my feet
Beneath the waterfall I'm complete

Flowing down into the Sea
Floating in the ocean free

As the sun sets over you
I stay and await you too

Trees cry leaves on to the forest's floor
The frost chills me… you are no more

Consumed by Darkness
I desperately seek the Light

Out of rhythm, out of time

I smell the flower come to life
Its' scent is carried by the night

I do not hear the eagle's cry
Yet the wind sings a lullaby

We are together you and I
Eternally we soar, we fly

2000

VL Parker

ANATHEMATIZED

The leaves are rotting on the ground above
The crows are circling the sky
I can't hear a sound

The worms are having a feast
A delicacy, as they dine
I can't feel inside

The sun is setting west of here
I no longer have to fear
I cannot see the light

The dank soil diminishes me
The body does decay
I have no choice

No light, no love
No song to be sung
I have no voice

Denounced and cursed
I lie anathematized

1984

AUTUMN LEAVES

From my childhoods first breath
I have not known love, but longed for Death

What others were before my helpless eyes…
In this world I could not help but despise

What others saw in me was less than impressive
As a sapling, life became oppressive

From my sorrow I could not awaken
Until I took the road seldom taken

The storms in my life slowly subsided
With each new dawn the discovery of self, coincided

The autumn leaves turned, to bright orange, red and a
hint of gold
Then in your gaze I began to fold

Your love saturated me like April showers
In our passion true love flowered

Love grew like the daffodils in spring
Now I wear your wedding ring
As we withstand the test of time
Our love ages like a good wine

I regret how short life can be
I curse Death; he is a thief

2011

Chains Around My Soul: Between Shadows & Light

BETWEEN LIGHT AND SHADOWS

Between light and shadows you will see my face
Between light and shadows the memories erased
Between light and shadows tell you where I've been
Between light and shadows I can now pretend

Shadows of my past creep along this face
Shadows of my past I wish I could erase
Shadows of my past never let me be
Shadows of my past haunt me now, you see

In the light I travel as the sun sets on my face
In the light I battle to obliterate
In the light I search everywhere for me
In the light I'm blinded someone help me see

2001

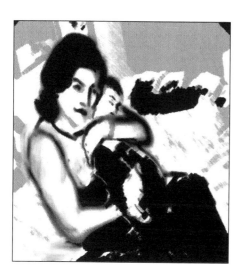

Chains Around My Soul: Between Shadows & Light

CAN YOU HEAR HIS VOICE

Standing at the water's edge
I can see your face
Shimmering in the distance
Beauty filled with grace

Stepping into the water
Kisses on my skin
Naked beneath waterfall
Wash away my sins

Listen to the Eagle's cry
Can you hear his voice?
Watching the bird circle me
Still I have a choice

Standing in your glory Lord
I fall to my knee
Claiming my own shield and sword
You have set me free

Reading the book in silence
I am lost here in your love
One day I will be with you
Forever in heaven above

2000

CHAINS AROUND MY SOUL

The blanket is black overhead
A cross tattooed upon my skin
I'm hanging from the tree
As the owl seeks its prey

The mouse shrieks shrill, it's dead
As blood drips on my wrist, a sin
I'm sitting here staring out to sea
The owl's perched above to stay

A pellet at my feet, the owl's fed
He lets out a victory cry, he wins
Weak and weary… he stares down at me
The chains around my soul… I pay… I pay

The Savior holds the key, I'm wed
The price was paid in blood, I'm in
I fall down on my knees
I pray.

I'm dead, I'm wed, I'm free, I win

No more chains for me my friend.
I win, I 'm in, I sin…

Chains around my soul again

1995.

VL Parker

FOLLOW ME

The morning's mist rolls across my ocean's bay
The sun is rising each and every day
The rains fall into the mountain's stream
My love flows through the world of dreams

No one cries for the children of the street
No one says a prayer for their souls to keep
No one gives them a coat to help them survive the cold
My little children I feel for your souls

Your tears run dry in this world of sin
You're always asking me where I've been
Your indifference blinds you to life beyond the ocean's door
I am in the wilderness of the streets and washed upon the shore

My life is unimportant to many in this world of gloom
My Father cared enough to place me in my mother's womb

My tears and blood were shed for all who question why
I will never hide, nor hang my head in shame to cry
No one sheds a single tear for our brothers and sisters of the night
No one gives them armor for the fight

No one knows how easy it will be if everyone
bears a little of the load

I am a ray of hope for those who cry and are
feeling low

Care a little and our tears will fall like   desert rain
Care a little and help life grow again
Care a little and you will see that it won't stop
I will rise again, high above the mountaintop

I am a light unto the world for everyone to see
I am the sun and the rain for all eternity
I am the sea, follow me

1990

Chains Around My Soul: Between Shadows & Light

VL Parker

GROWING GREY

You have given her nothing except a distortion of reality

Give her drugs and wish her well, while she awaits the dinner bell, finality

Christmas time she sits alone, trying to chew on stale scones, dunked in her tea

This was not what was meant to be

She taught you how to fly

She sang you that lullaby

And as you sit and dye your hair

She sits on drugs and stares

She held you up when life was rough

I guess you thought it wasn't enough

Now she waits idly by, too old to cry

Now a widow of life, prepared to die

She was a mother and a wife

Chains Around My Soul: Between Shadows & Light

That must have been another life

Now she looks up or maybe down

Doesn't matter when no one else is around, I frown

You haven't seen her in a long time

But when others ask you say she's fine

Then you go and dye your hair

Dreading the day that you'll be sitting there

Lost on drugs, left to stare

Stare, you stare

Then you go and dye your hair and hide the grey.

You say, "I'll go see her another day"

Afraid of what it will cost

Afraid of what is lost

But stop a visit her for a while and see

Death, is a certainty

Death Comes for you

He comes for me

So sit a while and stay

Don't be afraid of growing grey

2001

I WAIT FOR DEATH

&

DEATH WAITS FOR ME

My body is too weary

My soul is too old

My eyelids are too heavy

Peering through the window

I've been searching for you forever

I've been trying to escape

I've been fighting far too long

Every day I'm filled with hate

Too tired to drink the water

Too sick of longing for some sleep

Too lonely to bother crying

My life's still incomplete

VL Parker

I lay here upon the ground

I wait for Eternity

I wait For Death to kindly arrive

Must he wait for me?

1987

IF

If I had enough time in this world I would not be shy

I would walk along the beach and skinny dip at night

We'd make love in the sand and you would be my man

If I had more time I'd watch you as you sleep

I'd listen to you breathing soft and sweet

I'd wake you with a kiss, what a wish

If I had more time I would fly

I'd sing a song of passion

We would walk hand in hand

You would wonder why

I ran; I ran...

If I could

I would...

VL Parker

If

If, if, if, IF... I feel the sifting sand

So I now approach Eternity

I sit and wait, and wait, and wait

Death laughs at me when I fight

Still the Reaper will come

He now takes my hand

I hate commands

I lost Life

Alas

Pass

Please don't wait the grave is a finite place

The sands of time are flowing here tonight

Don't waste your life or you will fall from grace

If you summon up some audacity

Ignore the fear and numbness in your knees

Let the conversation slowly transpire

Delight in Life, in Love, and in the Light

For your life is short and time is not long

Kiss them as the dew kisses a flower

Don't say, "If only I had the power"

If, if, if, if... If I did not cower

Time is now up, your life has past the hour

If...

1987

INSIDE OUT

Inside I am Venus, goddess of love

Outside I'm a big mama and I huff and puff

Inside my kisses are succulent and sweet

Outside, "Wait while I floss my teeth"

Inside my skin is softer than a rose

Outside, "Forgive me Love while I use this pumice stone"

Inside I'm moist and wet

Outside… shriveled, dry and overfed

Inside I'm filled with vivaciousness

Outside, I sleep, no longer tenacious

Inside my hair is soft as silk

Outside it's a nest to lay eggs in

Inside I'm perfect in every way

Outside, oops, I just gained more weight

Yet here you are still with me as I remember who I used to be and still you love me inside out.

1994

Chains Around My Soul: Between Shadows & Light

VL Parker

NO LONGER YOUR APHRODITE

I use to be your Aphrodite

In some long forgotten dream

You were a prisoner of my passion

My girdle is now too small

Now I am your obligation

A duty you must fulfill

The proverbial ball and chain

Just a test of faith

I hold back tears in silence

As they fall like desert rain

Giving life to darkness

With no one left to blame

For I can't catch your eye

I no longer hold the key

We do not share a mind

You are no longer mine

I lay here in the darkness

I stare up at the moon

I see the stars shine above

Listening to the wind whisper words of love

2001

OCEAN BLUES

The ocean always makes me catch my breath

When the moon shines above I'm tied to life, to love

Waves lapping gently throughout the night give serenity

And when I catch sight of a pod of whales swimming by

I sigh, I sigh

I sit in sadness and contemplate their fate

As man contaminates their life

Destroyed by sewage, oils, and pesticides

I cry, I cry

The tides wash plastic and garbage upon the shore

The beauty is no more

I hear a dolphin laugh at me jumping high

See me, see me

I smile and pick up a bag and begin to clean the beach again

Perhaps the winds will change

I feel the storm clouds blowing in

The rage begins, begins

I hear the storm raging, fighting, crashing and bashing

With all its might it struggles to restore, renew

This world for me and you

Renew, renew...

Chains Around My Soul: Between Shadows & Light

VL Parker

ON MY OWN

Today I sit alone in the confines of my room

Trying to believe I enjoy this solitude

Alas I am afraid and lonely in the night

Of what, I do not know.

Today the music plays softly in my ear

A song of duty

A song a choice

A song of filled with fear

Outside the sun is shining

The birds are swift in flight

I sit quiet and alone

Waiting for the night

The week's too busy for you and I,

Walking toward the tomb

Still, I face the multitude

In our haste I see you briefly in the light

Once or twice we make love, but then you have to go

In the night I am content whenever you are near

Such beauty

Such a sweet surrender takes away the fear, as passion gives love and life a voice

My sad song has sung a final tune, but what about the timing?

I have no rhythm and no rhyme and yet here you are tonight

No longer on my own

In you I will delight

Here alone I lie

In the confines of my mind the darkness still does loom

Forever there's a feud

I get up to do the work that must be done ready for the fight

Appearing self-reliant, brave and oh so strong, and yet you still know

How I hate my fear

That life and love will become a duty

I may lose my voice, still there is a choice

I'll get up and make the coffee so I can pass this test while the sun's still shining

I know that you're the one and that this is right

I know that in your love I have lived and I've grown

Stop this stupid fight; I'm not alone, tonight

No longer on my own... Alone   1989

ONCE I WAS A LADY

Here she was a lady.

Quiet and refined

Now she is a woman

Tarnished deep inside

Here she was a kitten

White and oh, so pure

Now she is a raven

Ashen from within

Here she was an angel

A Dove just taking flight

Now she is a seagull

Dependent upon the winds

Once she was an eagle,

Majestic, strong and free

Now she is a prisoner

Of a Memory

Chains Around My Soul: Between Shadows & Light

PRISONER OF TIME

What is Time, but some fallacious pace?

He is a thief, a cheat, the one I hate

He silently creeps upon my face

Tis an invention of the human race

Prisoners we march in haste and greed

Lacking wisdom, I do not want to feed

Still my heart keeps beating like a drum

Oh Time, cursed time must we all succumb?

Alas our victory lies beyond the grave

For that is when time will begin to fade away

Then we all will traverse and transcend time and space

We will dance to an everlasting tune of rhythmic grace

An endless sea of love and truth that exceeds the galaxy

March to a different drum

Strike a brand new beat

Your own rhythm

Your own rhyme

It's time

Time

2001

VL Parker

REACHING FOR HIS HAND

When I was a baby reaching for his hand

The strength the power; I didn't know, I did not understand

I rode upon his shoulders for many an hour, yet I did not see

With what ease he always carried me

As I grew and we yelled, going head to head

I failed to understand where all this had led

When I was a woman he walked me down the isle

He had tears in his eyes; crying's not his style

Beginning of the end

Too late for us to mend

When I had a boy he was oh so ill

He could not hold my son; he had to take his pills

When my boy was two he helped his Papa from the car

Little did he know that would leave a scar

This man had carried me, now he cannot stand,

Except with aid of his grandson reaching for his hand

1995

REST IN PEACE

Father, I still am crying deep in the night

In the depth of my soul I know it isn't right

I should rejoice that you are released from this pain

Help me wash away the stain

At night I sit up and wait for you to come no more

Please come and knock upon my door

Let me know that I am safe

No more tears in your embrace

In the night I still tend to lie awake

I listen to the wind blowing across the lake

Listening to some long forgotten tune

You know, I was a child of the moon

I find myself longing for what could have been

Remembering how you envision me as a teen

Sorrow and tears were never your style

I'll be okay in a little while

I remember your laughter and a smile on your face

A memory I never want erased

I remember you singing with a bottle of wine

This is what I remember most of the time

The pain's still fresh

Thinking of decaying flesh

With memories I can't forget

Please wake me and tell me, "My dear don't fret."

Is there some strange power I could invoke?

Someone tell me it's just a cruel joke

You can't be gone

Tell me, Dad, that it's dawn

I remember when you used to say

"Rise and shine"

"It's a brand new day"

And everything was fine

Let me climb up on your knee

Sing to me as I fall asleep

About some mythical world and forgotten day

Chasing the terrible dreams away

Help me Daddy, I don't want to cry

Why do I return to that scared little girl inside?

Lashing out at all the injustice of this war

When darkness comes I feel like I'm three or four

Now instead of your gentle face, it is the darkness that I see

No embrace, no one's left to comfort me

The Heavens have taken you in haste

Eternal slumber, Rest in peace... lay in waste

I'll pray the Lord your soul to keep

As for me I'll stay awake listening to the wind, across the lake

Your songs are calling out to me

Yet I must let you be

Daddy Rest in Peace

Lawrence Bruce Cosgrove died too soon.

June 11, 1936-March 11th, 1996

RIDE LIKE THE WIND

Ride like the wind across the Western Plains

Hurry before you go insane

Ride like the wind until you find a home

No need to worry if you're all alone

Then when you stop to rest

Beneath the stars confess

Watch the clouds go by under desert skies

While the winds die down you ride

Ride like the wind and fly

Beneath the evergreen you died

Ride like the wind down by the sea

Across the horizon toward serenity

Ride like the Wind   1986

SALVATION'S COME

In you I find strength in my darkest hour

You give me hope to persevere, you are my strong tower

As darkness falls around me, your love provides me light

Without you by my side I would lose this fight

You opened up my eyes; before I was blind

I was trapped by shadows hidden in my mind

You freed my soul; the demons are gone, gone at last

You love equipped me to escape the past

Breaking the chains of ignorance, before I died out there on that road

You taught me wisdom while you lightened my load

Thank you for making me whole

Your love has saved my soul

My heart was cold as ice, until you chipped away the fear

The changes in me are shocking; I know when you are near

I thank the Lord above, for bringing back the sun

I know you are the one

They say that Love heals all wounds; you showed me this is true

Your love has healed me and made me feel like new

I know now, my salvation's come

My love you are the one

2001

SHADOWS OF MY MIND

My Eyes have seen the darkness

Straining in the light

My body survived the winter

Only to be burned by desert skies

My ears have heard the rainfall

Beating upon the grave

My nose has smelt the roses

Only to smell decay

My mouth has tasted honey

Alas it was bitter once inside

My eyes have closed to dream

Only to be revived

My body lay awake

In the darkness of the night

My mind hears the howling wind

Only to tell me to go outside

My lips smile as I watch the sunrise

Experience the dawn

My mouth runs dry

As clouds of gray roll by

I try to focus on our love

What I know is true

But when I do the shadows of my mind cloud over
me and you

Love, please see me through

1989

SOMETHING ISN'T RIGHT

I am searching for you Jesus; I am looking for the light

I am looking in the darkness, something isn't right

I am searching for you Jesus; I am looking for you Lord

But I have to tell you Father, I am weary and I'm sore

I see hunger, I see hatred, I see injury and pain

And though I keep on crying, I just can't stop the rain

I see anger and injustice all around the world

As my life has come undone I have nowhere else to run

I am searching for you Jesus; I've been looking all my life

I know that I am tired and I'm sick of this never-ending fight

I am searching on this journey, this journey we call life

And though I keep on trying, something isn't right

I seek the truth and find I've been lied to… tell me what else can I do?

And though I wake each morning, I feel my life is through

I am searching for you Jesus in this God forsaken place

Even though I know I'm tired, I have to run this race

I am thirsty for your message, but I just can't hear your voice

I am listening here in silence; it seems I have no choice

And though I keep on knocking I am thrown back in the war

I have no place to rest; I guess I'll curl up on the floor

I know I'm cold and hungry. Please Jesus, set me free

I know I am in bondage and I'm too blind to see

I'm a sinner and I'm lonely; I have been all my life

I grew up in the darkness; I'm a child of the night

But still I keep on trying, please tell me what else can I do?

I am lost here in the darkness; I think my life is through

Please help me Jesus; won't you take command?

And as I lay here dying, I am reaching for your hand

2001

Chains Around My Soul: Between Shadows & Light

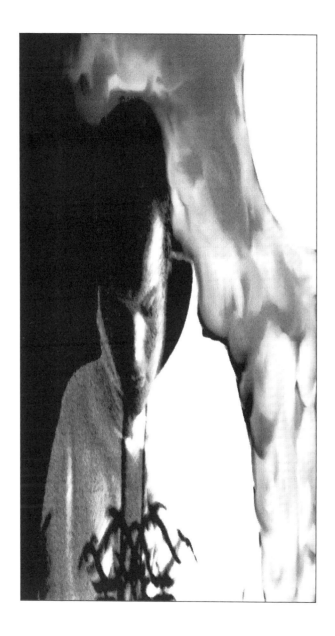

STANDING ON A PRECIPICE

How do I cope with these feelings inside?

A part of me, too hard to hide

Isolated and alone in pain

Tears a feeble attempt to shed the shame

Stranded upon the ocean blue

Wondering if only my life could be through

Clinging to this tiny host

If I survive, I'll need you most

Tossed carelessly upon the shore clinging to the rock in horror

Mesmerized by a precipice

Staring at the ocean mist

Something forces me to turn away

Supported by your wings, I pray

But still sometimes I stand and stare

I question, "Are you really there?"

Looking past my vacant soul

Into the Darkness below, no longer feeling whole

Staring off the Precipice

Above the Ocean's mist

"Step away!

"Step away…"

Live another day…

1996

TAKE A STAND

Declare who you are

Reach for the stars

Face the challenge and your fears

Even if it takes years and years

Take a stand!

Face what's wrong

Mommy is no longer there to urge you on

The war is waged; so take command

Go on take a stand!

Stop sitting quietly on the fence

Ignorance is no defense

Who can say what is right or wrong?

You can.

Come on, take a stand!

Exercise your right and fight.

Go on and reach great heights

Don't subjugate yourself under man

Take a stand!

Don't relegate yourself to the corner of the room

Too much can happen while you pout and fume

You'll sink in that sand, take my hand

Then go and take a stand!

What is foul? What is fair?

Use your voice and swear.

Obscenity is non-conformity?

It's your turn, Take a stand!

It's your life

Take Command!

Go on

Take a stand!

2000

THE HOUR'S PAST

A perfect child, a rose in spring, your praises we will always sing

As we grow we worship you, kneeling before our God and King

You smile and stare at me through the vastness of space and time

I see and hear you so clearly inside. "Child, you're mine."

My heart is beating, sharing in rhythm and rhyme

I count each breath and day until it's my time

You planted this seed in me long ago

I am so cold here beneath the snow

A white blanket shrouds me in your love

Still, I hear the crows' vile tune above

I don't recall when I left or how

I see the crow circling me now

My skin now decays here as I sleep

I say my prayers, still the bugs do creep

I do not know when I will be saved

I lay here waiting beneath the grave

Accepting that I don't hear the sound

Waiting for Life, or Death, to be found

Has my Lord abandoned me for all eternity?

Will I remain forever trapped in this wretched slumber?

No one can ever tell when Death shall call their number

Still heed this solemn warning to all of you from me

Enjoy life while it lasts for one day darkness falls

The curtain shall be drawn and Death will come to call

Time has had no meaning for a child of the moon

Life and Death, have their tune

Not you, nor I, will ever know the hour

Death knocks upon your door with power

He'll place an empty glass by you

Time for you to say adieu

Kneel and pray, alas

Knock, knock, knock, knock…

See the clock?

Farewell

Hell!

1997

THE ROAD I'VE TAKEN

I too came across that divergent road, but I had no one to share the load

I too was forced to choose

Without any hesitation I walked up to play and lose

It had a forest thick and deep and little light shone through

I stumbled often over a stone then my anger grew

I made my way through the heavy undergrowth, scratches on the skin

No one's here to wash away my sin

Someone once inquired as to my predicament

"No regrets" was my reply and I seldom wonder why, I went

But I believe that even if the grass were greener and the forest much less thick

The other side would've surely made me sick

Besides, my path provided places where no one else could see

At least I was free

You know those two paths still led me to that same place one day

They joined again and led me on my way

The path never changed what I'd become

It only let me hide as the dense forest muffled my cries, and I faced the setting sun

As I reach this journey's end I ask for no lamentation

I laugh because I reached my destination

I resign, not regretting that I chose a different road than most of you

That path forced me to bend beneath the trees and undergrowth, its true

I died a little every day

But I also grew along that way

Lay back years from now

Take your last deep breath and take a final bow

Never to go back again, except with the mind's eye

Lie beneath the Western sky

It settles down on you, your life is through

Death came for me now he comes for you,

Still, I learned, I grew, I laughed and loved and that's what life is all about.

I speak the truth, so have no doubt

Walk across that great divide

There's nothing left to hide

We enter into eternity naked and alone, but I know

Death is not the end

Just another step in our journey, friend

This is the Road I've taken

2001

Chains Around My Soul: Between Shadows & Light

WAR INSIDE OF ME

Raging fires inside my mind

Raging fires for all time

Raging fires in my heart

Raging fires in the dark

Raging fires I know not why

Raging fires I cannot hide

Burning passion sets me free

Burning passions let me be

Burning passions I lose control

Burning passions I am no more

Burning passions enhance life

Burning passions in the night

Cold veracity that brings the dawn

Cold reality that ends a song

Authenticity that balances life

Validity of what's right

Cold certainty destroys my soul

The truth is that I'm at war

1988

WHERE ONLY SHADOWS RESIDE

Churches crumble from within

Sicknesses of our very soul

Destroy the faith in sin

Shadows take control

Inside the mind

Inside the soul

We call out to find

Crying takes its toll

Washing hands

Washing feet

Standing on the sand

Sifted through like wheat

When will man ever learn?

We can't do it on our own

Salvation, we try to earn

Still, it comes beneath a heavy stone

Fall down on our knees to pray

Searching for his grace

Searching for a home some day

Alone, I see his face

I stand and walk, trying to decide

Looking for light to see

Where only shadows reside

In me

2001

WICKED

I was walking down the street, when I came upon this man.

He asked me, "What's your name my son?"

He was wondering who I am.

I said, "My name is Wicked, it's what they call me on the street."

Then he asked me if I wanted to know how to make my life complete.

I laughed and said, "You're kidding, tell me what's the scam?"

I stood a little straighter as I tried to look the man.

Then I continued slowly with a grin, "I may look young and foolish bro. but I've learned to live life thin."

He touched my shoulder gently as he smiled and said that he knows where I've been.

I saw a single tear in his eye as he shook his head and said, "You feel you have been to hell and back, in a corrupted world of sin."

"Oh I see you are a preacher." I laughed, "You're into saving souls."

Then I leaned back and relaxed as I lit my cigarette

Then I let him know, "That's really kind of bent."

"Let me teach you something brother," I told him with a look that was almost sincere, "This world is meant for dying, a cruel accident… and as for man, we are the earth's pestilence."

"I used to look for Jesus." I continued as I turned to look away, "You know my Ma and Pa didn't want me anyway…I made their life a mess.'

I shuffled my feet a bit and I let him in, "I ran away when I was nine, I guess I had enough."

I took a deep drag of my cigarette, "At least when a stranger hurts you, there is no illusion to the game. You no longer have the same reason to go insane."

"Blood's not thicker than water." I continued with a sigh, "…and as for that religious stuff, I really have had my fill. If I ever see another TV Evangelist I think I'll get ill. They promise to lead you to Jesus if you first help them pay their bills for a brand new BMW and their wife's new mink coat. Needless to say I didn't board that boat."

But as I ranted he calmly shook his head and appeared to agree, so I continued on and pleasantly recalled, "There was this one preacher, I used to listen to on the street. He talked about the book of Revelation, that was kind of neat."

Then I put my cigarette out as I noted the reality, "You know preacher, if this Jesus came on earth today, I have to tell you brother, I don't know anyone he would save, especially me."

I was compelled to confess some things that I've done, "Don't waste your time, I've cheated and I've lied. You know I've stolen lots of times. You have to, to survive."

"You are right about one thing preacher." I said with honesty, "I have been to hell and back again, tell me whatever did I do?"

I kicked a can on the ground and said, "You probably think they call me Wicked because of all the bad things I've done."

I looked down, then I confessed, "Maybe to a small degree that is really true…"

I laughed, "I admit some of it was fun, but they really call me, Wicked, you know, as in 'cool.'"

He smiled at me and touched my hand. It kind of frightened me; then he spoke, "I know that you've fed your brothers and sisters. You help them survive the streets. You clothe them when it's cold outside and help them find a place to get a good night's sleep. You tend to them when they're sick, and that's why they call you Wicked, son. You're almost complete."

"Almost!" I said, as he began to walk away.

His voice was carried like a whisper on the wind, "Follow me!"

I followed him to the beach and reached out for his hand, as I suddenly realized He left no footprints in the sand.

2001

YESTERDAY'S CHILD

Grey clouds swirling in my mind

Nothing changes over time

Tornadoes remembered from long ago

I was a child, I didn't know

Blood stain seeping through my soul

Some things never seem to change or go

We fool ourselves to think we'll grow

It's just a cruel illusion that we've gained control

Still the little girl that I used to be

Wishing Daddy was home to protect me

Crying out for freedom in the night

Knowing somehow this isn't right

Knowing, screaming, yelling, silently

Haunted by the shadows of my mind, everything I've seen

Slithering across time and space, a fiend

Reaching for the cross in haste I scream

Cursed, dirty, still unclean and damned

Hurry... Go and wash your hands!

1989

YOU ARE

You are heaven to me

You are the air I breathe

You are the ocean and the sea

You are the eagle that flies above

You are my trumpeter swan, my Love

You are the wolf howling with the wind

You are the ocean breeze against my skin

You are the sun and the moon

You are the North Star that guides me in

You are my heart and soul,

You are the one who makes me whole

You are my lover and my friend

Chains Around My Soul: Between Shadows & Light

You are the wind, which makes me bend

You are the Orca calling out to me

You are the one with whom I ascend

You are my heaven on earth

Every day I bless your birth

So today I thank the stars above

For giving you to me, My Love

1999

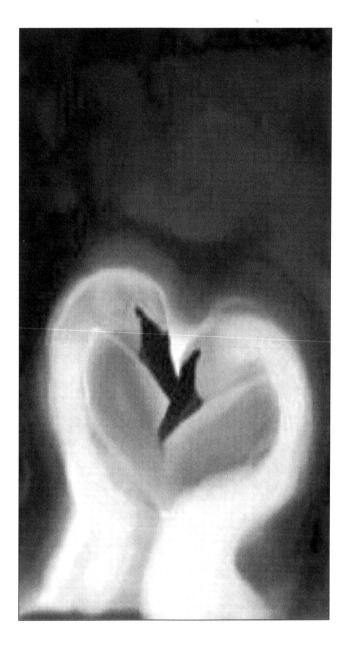

Chains Around My Soul: Between Shadows & Light

VL Parker

ZENITH

I have reached my zenith with you

Your love has pulled me through

Through the torrents and the storms

Our love has made me whole

They have said that true love heals, its true

I would never have made it without you

Without you by my side I would have lost control

Your love rescued me

You promised and we flew

High above this world and then I knew

We reached our Zenith, Love

Your love traversed the stormy sea

Your kisses are like the morning dew

Without you I don't know what I'd do

True love has healed and renewed my soul

I am now complete in soul

I'm whole, I whole

2013

ABOUT THE AUTHOR

VL Parker is a Literary Artist. She is an author, a poet, and an aspiring screen writer. She has already published her novel, **To Hell & Back A Test of Faith** and is preparing her second book in the series entitled, **When Angels Walk the Earth: The Rise of the Nephilim,** for publication in the Fall of 2013. Parker is also editing a series of screenplays adapted from her novel series.

Although VL loves photography, painting and other abstract artistic endeavors, her consuming passion is creative writing, of which poetry was her first artistic love. Verna-Lynn acknowledges that God, Robert and poetry delivered her from darkness and set her soul free. Although she feeds her passion for all forms of artistic expression, creative writing is particularly cathartic for this author.

Parker wrote poetry initially as method to deal with the emotions of a difficult childhood. It enabled her to utilize imagery and symbolism to express secret pain that she was too young and unwilling to address openly. Rather than keep a diary growing up VL wrote poetry to battle dark and foreboding thoughts that would have surly consumed her had she not had this outlet. Verna-Lynn also recognizes that she has always been spiritual and feels that both her relationship with God and the love of her husband play a monumental part of her healing and growth through the years.

VL met her high school sweetheart, Robert, in the fall of 1987 and they have three beautiful and gifted children. Matthew the oldest has designed both covers of his sister, Sarah C.E. Parker's, novels, **Flames of the Ether** & her new **book Realm of Night: Shadow of Destiny**. Sarah is a talented author, singer and song writer. She, like her sister Jessica, loves acting as well. Jessica is an exceptional singer and musician who writes her own songs and music. Jessica's beautiful voice and passion for both singing and acting have enabled her to perform major roles in several musicals. Both Parker girls have acted and sung in plays since they were three years old.

VL has always encouraged her children to, "***Dare to dream and rise above.***" She is now living out this in her own life. Parker has also chosen to live by another motto which is, "***Create without worrying about the opinion of the critics. Generate from the heart and soul and it will always reflect something unique and beautiful.***"   VL Parker

This dictum's message, are words that this Literary Artist is determined to live by and fervently hopes that her children will do the same. Still, there is an undeniable part of her soul that hopes that their art is appreciated and valued by others. It is in the midst of these mixed emotions that she wrote the following poem and leaves you to be the judge. It is a work that she wrote several years ago entitled,

"Parenthetical"

Verna- Lynn Parker now sends her first compilation out into the Universe and to you.

Enjoy

I leave you all with this final poem to ponder and look forward to hearing from you on my Facebook page, http://www.facebook.com/pages/VLParker/275296059195303

"PARENTHETICAL"

By the way I have something to say
I want to tell you before I forget
Incidentally, you don't have to agree
But I question, what is poetry?

Is it Prose?
Must it rhyme?
Should it rhyme only sometimes?
No one seems to agree on
What is poetry?

Must it be the language of the soul?
Should it let you in my mind?
I don't know what you would find
No one seems to understand
What is poetry?

While we are on the subject I would like to say
I have an opinion anyway
I want to tell you before you go that I do not know
What is poetry?

It is music to the ear
It is the language transcending years
It is a language of the soul
By and by it tends to open up the mind
Parenthetically is this poetry?

VLP 2001

Chains Around My Soul: Between Shadows & Light

Poetry is a soul's song

Poetry is...

> "To thine own self be true."
>
> William Shakespeare